Seasons

A collection of seasonal reflections and poems

Café Writers, Derby Cathedral

© Copyright 2021 Derby Cathedral Café Writers Group

All rights reserved.

No part of this publication may be reproduced, stored in a retrieval system, or transmitted, in any form or by any means, electronic, mechanical, photocopying, recording or otherwise, without the prior written permission of the publisher.

British Library Cataloguing in Publication Data.
A catalogue record for this book is available from the British Library.

ISBN 978 086071 874 1

A Commissioned Publication Printed by

MOORLEYS
Print, Design & Publishing
info@moorleys.co.uk • www.moorleys.co.uk

The views, thoughts, and opinions expressed in this book belong solely to the author, and do not necessarily reflect the views of the publisher or any of its associates.

Seasons

A collection of seasonal reflections and poems

Café Writers, Derby Cathedral

edited by
April McIntyre

Contents:

Foreword 6

Introduction 7

Prologue: *Tree-time* — Richard Palmer — 9

Winter

Wintering	Christine Statham	14
In our hearts	April McIntyre	15
Let's G L O this Christmas	Maureen Burke	17
A song of praise	Rachel Kenning	19
Ducks on ice	Martha White	20
This is the dying time	Penny Young	22
Snowscape	Sharon Fishwick	23
Haiku	Sharon Fishwick	24
Cold, icicle cold	Raymond Lunt	25
Winter warmers	Ruth Allen	26
The call of the sea	Des Haigh	28
A journey in the snow	Chris Morris	30
Haiku	Sharon Fishwick	31
'Good for the garden'	Arnie Rainbow	32
That which was lost	Anna Marley	34
Haiku	Sharon Fishwick	35

Spring

Is it really spring?	Sharon Fishwick	38
Lent is for life	April McIntyre	39

Sprightly spring	Amanda Cartwright	41
New life in the garden	Arnie Rainbow	43
Beautiful moment	Mary Martin	45
New life after death	Margaret Stevens	46
Spring in lockdown	Sharon Fishwick	48
Liminal space	Nicola Wong	49
'Silent spring'?	Arnie Rainbow	50
New life	Rachel Kenning	52
Spring flowers	April McIntyre	53
It's springtime	Raymond Lunt	54
A kind of awakening	Eirene Palmer	56
Spring in my steps	Mary Mills	58
Camping in spring	Rachel Kenning	60
Silver Mount in spring	Sharon Fishwick	62

Summer

Childhood summers	Rachel Kenning	65
Looking forward to summer 2020	Amanda Cartwright	67
Time	Sharon Fishwick	68
Summertime	Arnie Rainbow	69
Open garden Sunday	Raymond Lunt	71
Summer's evening at Carsington	Rachel Kenning	73
Summer haiku	Mary Mills	74
	Sharon Fishwick	74
	April McIntyre	74
In meadows greet the summer	Clare Merry	75

Crimson sunrise	Mary Martin	77
Water of life	Arnie Rainbow	78
Too hot to move	April McIntyre	80
Closer to me	Mary Martin	81
Last of the summer days	Raymond Lunt	82
Summer prayer: the gift of silence	Nicola Wong	84
Farewell to Summer	Sharon Fishwick	86

Autumn

Extravagance	Martha White	89
Haiku	Nicola Wong	90
Making chutney	April McIntyre	91
Autumn glory	Raymond Lunt	93
Blessings on the breeze	Rachel Kenning	95
Geese over the river	Rachel Kenning	96
Ode to Autumn	Eirene Palmer	98
Conker	Desmond Haigh	100
Downsizing	Ruth Allen	101
Weathering the storm	Arnie Rainbow	103
Pensees	April McIntyre	105
Changes	Arnie Rainbow	106
Spider!!	Lisa Ollerenshaw	109
Autumn prayer	April McIntyre	110
Remember, remember	Amanda Cartwright	111

Acknowledgements   113

Foreword

I am very pleased that Derby Cathedral hosts the Café Writers Group. Affiliated to the Association of Christian Writers, it is one of the largest Christian writing groups in the country and is much valued within our cathedral community.

Words are important to people of faith. *'In the beginning was the Word,'* writes St John. Through the Word all things were made. The use of words and their creativity takes us to the heart of what it is to be human and therefore to the heart of what it is to understand God and God's relationship to the natural world.

We can treasure this wonderful collection of writings as an expression of humanity and its creativity, especially in our relationship with the seasons and nature. Put words alongside art and photographs and you are in for a stimulating experience. The ability to express the human response to creation in all its variety is so evident in what you will read and see.

I hope that this collection will be shared widely and, as the prose and poetry is read by ever-increasing circles, that others will be inspired to put pen to paper in an equally creative manner.

The Very Rev'd Dr Peter Robinson, Dean of Derby

Introduction

When we started Café Writers at Derby Cathedral in 2017, we had little idea of the enthusiasm and talent that this writing group would yield. Then, one day, someone said, 'Why don't we publish some of our work so that others can enjoy it?' The result was a project to produce *Seasons*, a book of reflections on the annual changes that we all live through.

The seasons affect us greatly. The changing tides of rain and sun; the shifting patterns of shade and light on the landscape; plus that occasional white coat of wintry solitude, move us. There is something elemental and soulful about the seasons and if we pause for a reflective moment, this can stir us somewhere deep within.

We hope that you will find something in this book to help you stop and give thanks to God for the wonderful world in which we live. We have a precious gift that we all need to care for and cherish, especially in these troubling times of climate change.

Books don't just happen, however. Sincere thanks go to all of our writers who have contributed their work, art and photographs to the making of this book. A special thank you goes to April McIntyre who has worked tirelessly to edit and format the raw materials to create our first book in its finished form. Thank you, April.

Eirene and Richard Palmer
Leaders of Café Writers
September 2021

...like a tree planted by streams of water, which yields its fruit in season and whose leaf does not wither.
Psalm 1: 3

Prologue: Tree-time
Richard Palmer

Winter

Hibernation. This is the start of my year. I love the respite. My upper world is blessed with the wind, the rain and the cold. This is my time of fitness training. The elements strengthen me. Wind buffets my boughs and branches. I bend and twist and grow strong, thickening my sinews. I shed the dead wood that I no longer need. The sharp frosts make me resilient. I stand proud and untouched by them. And I give shelter to many within myself – the insects and mammals and birds that roost and hide and sleep along with me. The days are short. The world is darker. This is my time to take stock.

And I start to ruminate that soon, deep down, I must put out more roots. The winds remind me, 'Dig deep if you are to grow mighty. Go, find new strength within your subterranean depths. Seek out more. Find new sources to nourish you. Become more grounded in God's bottomless earth. Be unyielding and strong.'

What a glorious time this is.

Spring

Awakening. The sap begins to rise. I feel an overwhelming sense of new life and gratitude. This is my drug, the hormones and blood that floods through every fibre and tendril of my being, a message to every part of me to wake up and rejoice, for there are many things to do. Buds form and new growth spurts out of me.

I branch out in new directions, spreading myself, growing and creating. All my strengthening work and rootedness is paying off. A new season is upon me and it is time to turn over many new leaves. More light, more life, more vigour.

Summer

Fruitfulness. It all happens so quickly, the metamorphosis of greening and leafing. Twigs sprout, fruit and seeds burst forth from me. I am pollinated and blessed. There is so much to do. Long days of radiant light bring all the choicest things out of me. My crown shines in glory.

I host. The birds nest. The squirrels raise their young. The insects whirr and buzz within me. It is a time of happiness. And new life springs forth and dances.

I give away my seed and fruit. I drop some around me. They say that the fruit never falls far from the tree. And so it is with me. I have some of my family here close by, growing and putting down their own roots. Others are carried away by my friends, the animals, the birds, to explore new lands. Like all seed, only a little will survive. But that is nature's way. It works well and I know they will carry on my good work elsewhere.

Autumn

Meditation. I reflect on my year. My second transformation begins. I shed my leaves and some late seed. I have brought up the goodness of the earth from the depths and now return it to the soil, spreading a duvet of leaves beneath me. This replenishment is one of my gifts to the world. It nourishes and protects my neighbouring plants and trees. We look out for one another and each other's children. It is a system of mutual care, thousands of seasons in the making, a joint enterprise of cherishing and nurturing.

There are many creeds among us. Some love this rich nutritious soil and the valleyed woodland in which I grow. Others like the heat and a sparser life. For some it is rocky places, sandy soils, cold climates. We are all different. But without one another, we cannot live. We are harmonious towards each other, for it is by this means that tree-time goes on and on, never wavering in its common divine purpose.

My seasons are hibernation, awakening,
fruitfulness and meditation.
I relish them and I thank God for them.

Winter

Wintering
Christine Statham

Red sun setting
Morning frosting
Thermal vest adorning
Scarf entwining

Winter approaching
Darkness descending
Curtains drawing
Lights glowing

Beef stewing
Pies filling
Custard comforting
Tummies gurgling

Coal fire glowing
Hot chocolate warming
Old films entertaining
Winter lazing

Candles flickering
Lightness brightening
Spring beckoning
Kindling hope

In our hearts
April McIntyre

We sit amongst dusty boxes untangling the Christmas lights. December is underway and there's still so much to do. As devastation gives way to decoration, I venture into the soggy outdoors, returning with a dripping armful of greenery: holly, actually adorned with berries this year, ivy and rosemary, adding vibrancy to the ornaments and candles carefully arranged over the fireplace. A pungent, aromatic smell lingers on my fingers.

Upstairs in the study, I also prepare my worship area. It's just the top of a short bookcase where I usually place pebbles, candles and objects to look at or hold as I pray, changing them according to season or mood. In this time of Advent, I take the cross away and create instead a simple scene with two figures: an angel and a girl, Mary. Kneeling in the flickering candlelight, this will take me all the way from Nazareth to Bethlehem and beyond as I enter once again into the ancient story.

Now, on the edge of my minimal nativity, I add a sitting, reflective figure. She gazes at Mary and watches the unfolding drama, still but attentive. I find it comforting to know that, while I am dashing through my list of jobs or tearing my hair out as the pressures mount, she remains, holding my unspoken prayers and yearnings. Last Christmas, I felt I needed to move this figure, this 'little me', closer, to sit next to Mary and her baby, no longer an observer but drawn into the very circle of God's love.

There are many situations, particularly at this time of the year, when we think about the needs around us and the people we love and words seem so inadequate. Yet, like Mary, we can 'treasure up all these things' in the stillness, knowing that we are held in God's love, not just for Christmas but for always.

*Mary treasured up all these things
and pondered them in her heart*
Luke 2: 19

Let's G L O this Christmas
Maureen Burke

In the midst of adversity,
gratitude is a mere strip of hay in the middle of a needle stack,
painfully hard to find.
It's the last thing on your mind.
As we fight the coldness
of homelessness
and try to soothe the relentless
pangs of hunger,
at the blink of an eye, hunger
transforms into anger.

SO
Let's GLO this Christmas to cultivate an attitude
of gratitude
to surf the tsunami of adversity.

As the storm of hatred
rages within four walls,
threatening to shred
Homes. Workplaces. Schools. Communities.
When SELF threatens to explode like a Molotov cocktail

Let's GLO this Christmas and rise above
the storm like a dove,
a symbol of peace and love,
sprinkling the joy of love within
Homes. Workplaces. Schools. Communities.

In the midst of sufferation,
isolation
offers its warm embrace.
As no man
could understand
the depth of his brother's pain,
only he who feels it knows it.
But - we are our brother's keepers.
We are our sister's keepers.
We are one.

SO
Let's GLO this Christmas
to cultivate an attitude of sameness
of oneness
to lighten each other's load.

Let's GLO this Christmas.
Let's fire up our passion
like a steam train gathering momentum
as it snakes through the mountains of excesses
and the valleys of wants.

Let's GLO this Christmas.
A radiance of Gratitude. Love. Oneness.
Let's grow and glow and grow that flicker into a flame.
Let's GLO every minute.
Let's GLO every day.
Let's GLO every year.
NOT JUST AT CHRISTMAS.

A song of praise
a poem to read aloud
Rachel Kenning

I smell the silent air of frozen ponds, of glitter-spangled
pavements on the cold, winter morning, while the sun
sings its song of praise to skeletal branches on stately trees
transformed

into crystal, beautiful priceless treasures of diamonds and gems.
I am transported into a fairy tale woodland, sparkling
like tinsel, a winter wonderland of evergreens
glistening

with frost on fallen logs, beech nuts and cones, spider webs and
feathery pines dusted in white powder. I crackle my way over
crunchy mud, through transparent leaves and past dead flowers
suspended

in time like icy forest folk waiting for spring to come again,
to sing their song of praise in the strange silence of the wood.
Anticipating the joy and wonder of new life,
looking

across at the derelict cottage, its frost-laden windows of
flowers and ferns. Icicles hanging from gutters,
hungry black birds stealing berries,
blood red

against sprinkling of sparkling white powder on a landscape
stretching to infinity. I look far and wide, exhilarated
on this wonderful winter morning
singing a song of praise.

Ducks on Ice
Martha White

The air was cold but the sky was blue, the kind of blue that lifts your heart up to touch the puffy clouds sailing high overhead. The sun lit up the bare spindly branches of the trees and the bleached winter grass and turned the water's surface into shining silver. We stood on the muddy bank, hands jammed in our coat pockets, and giggled.

The lake in front of us was half-frozen, and watching the ducks was hilarious. They paddled along perfectly happily in the water, but as soon as they got onto the ice their poise deserted them. Their webbed feet slid out in all directions, depositing them on their tails, and every now and then the solid surface would give way underneath them, leaving them suddenly bobbing back in the water. If one tried to get up onto the ice, it involved a good deal of flapping and splashing. Bits of ice kept breaking off, leaving the flustered duck floundering, but determinedly coming back for another go.

A long-toed moorhen was picking its way carefully underneath an overhanging tree, like a novice ice skater sticking close to the edge of the rink. Out in the middle, the more confident ducks were pretending to be experts – until suddenly they weren't and landed on their tails again.

It was funny to us, but we wondered what the ducks thought about this wintry change. Were they frustrated or angry that the water wasn't behaving as it should? Did they worry that the lake would never be the same again?

Often, when things change, we feel like those ducks: suddenly unsteady where previously we had been confident. We struggle to make sense of our new reality. And we don't appreciate people standing at the edges and laughing at us!

But sometimes, as we find our balance on a slippery surface, we gain a new depth to our life and faith. We can start to understand better these lines from a famous poem in the Bible:

God is our refuge and strength,
a very present help in trouble.
Therefore we will not fear,
though the earth should change,
though the mountains shake in the heart of the sea.
Psalm 46: 1-2 (NRSV)

So, even when the world changes around us and we fall on our tails yet again, we can look up to the blue sky and find a hope that is greater than our fear.

This is the dying time
Penny Young

Now the hedgerow
Is blanched for an hour with transitory blossom
Of snow, a bloom more sudden
Than that of summer.

T. S. Eliot, <u>Little Gidding</u>

Surely the Spring, when God shall please,
Will come again like a divine surprise.

Charlotte Mew, <u>May 1915</u>

This is the dying time.
Branches are bare, leaves fallen,
the earth hugs itself
and the spirits of creatures shrink,
fold themselves against the cold.
Now the hedgerow is blanched for an hour
with transitory blossom of snow.

Snow falls – fake blossom,
foreshadowing the coming of spring –
a bloom more sudden than that of summer
and melting away as quickly as it came
from its temporary place,
leaving room for the fruitful flowers of spring
which, pushing through the mulch of dead things,
will come again, and again, and again
like a divine surprise, like refreshing rain.

Snowscape
Sharon Fishwick

A snow bunting, scoops
clear of the ground, perching
on the glistening granite boulder,
the wind tossing its call
into the abyss below.

A white landscape flows
down from the corniced ridge.
Plumes of drifting snow
fly high into the swirling air,
icy dust choking every gasp of breath.

We stop by streams, halted abruptly
as the temperature plummets
in the depths of a blue night.
Icy fingers reach down
from outstretched branches laden with snow.

Reindeer lie, calm and content,
antlers and faces plastered,
with a white, soft mask
carefully placed by the brittle north wind,
the search for lichen halted.

Soon the storm will pass.
Then clicking heels, the only sound
of a herd on the move again,
through the deep mountain snow
following the herders call.

A crack of branches
icy fingers reach down low
heavy snow falling

Haiku by Sharon Fishwick

Cold, icicle cold
Raymond Lunt

Cold, icicle cold,
as bitter winds blow wild,
reaching deep into the bones.
Snow lies heavily on roofs and roads,
white with winter freshness;
but cold, icicle cold.

Cold, icicle cold:
the feelings deep inside
as a loved one passes on.
Alone with grief and memories
on empty winter nights,
bereft of touch, now gone.

Comes the melting sun,
warming the earth with hope,
promising new life in Spring,
and love from friends and church and God
lights up the darkest place
until new hope is born.

Winter Warmers
Ruth Allen

'I've never been in this situation before. And it's only been a week. I've always worked. What do I do when this project finishes?'

Liz takes off her sodden coat, shakes the snow from her woollen hat and looks around the room. Bill is snoring on the floor. One man is rocking to and fro, clearly agitated. Yanek is on his phone speaking Polish. Some are with the outside door volunteers having a chat and a smoke. (The door volunteers refuse entry to known trouble-makers.)

We are at the churches' night shelter for the homeless. Some volunteers are cooking and serving a hot meal, others are engaging with the guests. There is banter and laughter and calls for more pudding with custard. I bring Liz a dinner and Yanek comes to show me his phone. 'Old phone stolen. Photos gone.' He shows me a boiler. 'I fix. No leak. Certificate for course on old phone. Gone.'

'Where is the original certificate?' I ask. A shrug. He lifts both hands in the air. 'No place to keep.' Of course! He's homeless.

I hear more from Liz. Scared and frustrated, she explains she lost her job, is waiting for benefits, and has now lost her flat. I ask if she has been to the daytime venue for advice. 'Yes. I went today and they want me back tomorrow. They may be able to help.' So, a shred of hope.

The night staff arrive. We evening volunteers gather for a debrief and a prayer for the thirty-four guests asleep on camping mats.

So, as we reflect on our response to the homeless sitting in doorways during the day, we could say hello and bring a coffee. We could check websites for homeless charities and see if there is a way we could be involved or help financially.

It's a privilege, though, to hear the stories and to share a chuckle from time to time. Our current project, which is open every winter night, closes at the end of March.

My prayer for the guests who come into the winter warmth is that solutions are found and I give thanks for all the volunteers who make night shelter possible.

Names and stories used above are not those of actual people.

The Call of the Sea
Des Haigh

She stood entwined in her own darkness.
I stood close by, clutching my bottle of substitute freedom,
two closeted slaves of society, broken free from our chains,
seeking refuge on our vast solitude beach,
staring out into the night as it bends to kiss the winter sea:
a writhing body, veiled blue upon black, lost in some
distant horizon to the black velvet gown of the sky.

The grime of the city, still sick in our blood,
and the return to the prison of crippling convention
hung inerrant and dogmatic in our painful consciousness
like an unmerciful enemy advancing our flank.

I threw back my head, seeking my real self in each purposeful
drink,
absorbing the heaving sea, sucked by the unseen moon,
and the sight of two seagulls lying dead;
soft-boned feathers shrouded by the wind-blown sand,
waiting to be gathered-in to the soul of the sea,
to fly a spiritual flight, bathed by denser currents.

Her own eyes were held silently spellbound by the pulsing tide,
sperm surf surging endlessly to the welcoming womb
and a white marbled break rising from the sea's crutch
pushed deep in the belly of the widespread sand,
straddled by the tide thrusting like moist white hips.

She moved, then, gently down the thighs of the soft wet sand,
allowing the sea's freedom to caress her erect limbs
and fully embraced by the wild winter wind,

swirling like impassioned fingers through her dark hair.
She pressed deeper into the stroking surf,
wanting to be lost to wanton freedom.
Her eyes braced the heavens, consenting the sea to take her
as the tide rolled in like one big tear,
until at last my loving hand reached her arm,
then led her sadly from the beckoning sea whisper,
back to the emptiness.

A journey in the snow:
observations during a snowy, February walk in the Derbyshire Dales

Chris Morris

Farmer with horses and fields,
scarf on his face and boots down below in the snow.

Long-tailed tits, balance on wiggly twigs
sending soft showers on bushes below in the snow.

Yellow sheep, scrape, hungry for breakfast,
through hedgerow and pasture below in the snow.

Trees stacked, white shouldered branches
drop their loads on tyre tracks below in the snow.

Bench draped like a three-tiered wedding cake;
memory plaque of walkers in shadows below in the snow.

Distant Dales wrapped in cold, crisp blankets:
duvets for bulbs and spring flowers below in the snow.

Frost's white spears sparkle in woodland rays;
silent thawing, onto brittle bracken below in the snow.

Meadow's haven for robins, wrens, tits, goldfinch, magpies,
crows and blackbirds seeking worms below in the snow.

Broken shack, like unfulfilled dreams, and a child's death.*
Half brick walls, rusty, corrugated sheets in muck below in the snow.

Rippling river sparkles over shiny black pebbles;
clear dark pools for Grey Heron below in the snow.

Neighbours, warm fires, fragrance of curry,
building snowmen, shovelling paths below in the snow.

See nature's wonders, blankets and birds in winter;
earth's resting stillness, our lesson below in the snow.

* <u>The Shack</u>, William P. Young, 2007

Wise trees stand sleeping
snow blossom falls from heaven
winter's solitude

Haiku by Sharon Fishwick

'Good for the garden'
Arnie Rainbow

We all love a good grouse about the cold. Maybe it's because we're an island nation but we're never happier that when we're talking about the weather. One-to-one with a stranger, the 'ice-breaker', if you'll excuse the pun, is usually along the lines of 'Cold as a reindeer's nose, ain't it?' - or perhaps something more colourful!

Mind you, the cold has its upsides. My dad swore that neither parsnips, nor sprouts were worth eating until they had been well-frosted. Later, as a botany student, I learnt that freezing weather triggers conversion of the plant's stored starch into sugar to fuel a burst of spring growth. So chilled veg. really does taste sweeter. Many plants have seeds that need a spell of freezing weather to trigger germination, while others need a chill to stimulate flowering. So, no winter freeze, no spring growth!

Water is unique in that, as it freezes, it *expands*. The expansion force is so great that water, trapped within cracks, breaks down rocks into tiny fragments, hence the scree on mountain sides. It's a key stage in the creation of soil. Without this anomaly, life on the land would be very limited: no soil means no vegetation and thus no animal life and no human life. Of course, good soil is much more than mineral matter: it also contains the remains of dead plants and animals, plus a huge assortment of beneficial microbes and tiny creatures.

Jesus of Nazareth must have been aware of the importance of good soil. As a carpenter's son he would have often rubbed shoulders with farmers. His parable of the sower reflects this. The seed that fell on stony ground was short-lived, whereas the good soil provided enough water and nutrients to grow a good crop. Of course, Jesus wasn't lecturing on agriculture! By 'seed', he meant his *word*: his teaching about the new life that he was offering. Just as some soils are stony and barren, so some of us have 'stony hearts', whereas others are like the good soil that nurtured the seed and grew a bountiful crop, yielding more seed, more life for everyone.

The relationship between seed and soil remains a conundrum. Freezing weather and death help form good soil; both support new life. Even the seed has to 'die', creating new life that multiplies over and over again. So why should we fear winter when it's just the precursor to spring and new growth. Why fear death when it's just a step towards new life.

That which was lost
Anna Marley

Looking out we spied him
from our back gate,
darting in a blizzard
and it seemed too late.
Climbing undeterred,
muffler on the ground,
to find that distant bleating,
crying to be found.

He went to such trouble
all for one sheep,
coming to our door,
his joy running deep.
We invited him in
to share a cup of tea,
opening our hearts
immediately.

The shepherd left the ninety nine
to show his love to one.
Our God will do the same for us
through Jesus Christ, his Son.

The early sunrise
wakening snowdrops bow heads
glory to our Lord

Haiku by Sharon Fishwick

Spring

Is it really spring?
Sharon Fishwick

The wind whips the cat flap
clicking, clattering but he doesn't step through.
He's too wise in his old age
to venture out into this storm.

Rain, in too much of a hurry,
lashes against the windows
its claws screeching against the glass,
unrelenting external anger.

Rivers rising, yet again.
Floods are old news now
perpetuating the damage and loss
caused by last week's storms.

The calendar insists this month is spring.
Tulip heads splayed with heavy water globules;
daffodil stalks bend, flowers bowing heads:
a prayer for repentance in Lent.

With His help, we look forward to sunny days
and new life skipping around the fields.
The farmer, busy looking after his flock,
as our Lord takes care of His.

Lent is for life
April McIntyre

Is it spring yet? I'm feeling restless urges to clean cupboards, plant seeds, put on walking boots and tramp the hills, wear bright colours and eat salads. Shall I respond? Perhaps a coffee and chocolate biscuit first!

Oh no! I've given up chocolate for Lent! Joined the thousands of devout but rather sad chocoholics embarked on forty days of fasting, counting down the days to Easter Sunday when we lavish our joy on a mountain of Fairtrade chocolate. Is this what fasting is all about? Yet who can take Lent seriously when cream eggs and hot cross buns have been on sale since Boxing Day?

Surprisingly enough, quite a few Christians do take Lent seriously. Lent is for life not just for chocolate. It's a great time to enter imaginatively into the story of Jesus as he makes his lonely way into the Judean desert, praying, wrestling with thoughts, tested to the limits, until he emerges with renewed purpose to share his revolutionary vision of God's kingdom. If we walk with him as the weeks unfold, we will finally enter Jerusalem amidst the shouts and waving palm branches, share a last supper, agonise with him in the garden and, perhaps, be there with him, in the darkness, as he cries out his love on the cross.

Many people meet up in churches or homes to study and reflect over Lent. Some make space in the diary to attend retreats and quiet days, hoping to discern that 'still, small voice' of God. Others give up on 'giving things up' and instead try to do one positive thing in the community each day: sharing a smile, making someone a drink at work, offering a lift to a neighbour.

Little things that help make God's love real.

Lent is a chance to brush away the cobwebs and try a spiritual make-over, responding to the God who calls to us as creation comes alive again.

Lent is for life not just for chocolate. Bring it on!

Sprightly spring
Amanda Cartwright

'We've all got a spring in our step,' my friend said.

I knew what she meant, even though the bright, blustery skies of March were weeks away. A word of encouragement had been spoken, a new voice heard and a discreet moment of kindness shared in the candlelit evening church. There was a stirring in our hearts which promised that the months of lonely, unaided struggle hadn't been in vain, that tears of grief will turn to gladness and our tired feet will find their bounce again. Yes, there will be another spring.

The season of spring really does what it says, bouncing into the cold year with a loud 'boing'! As the sap rises, as green shoots break through the cold earth and leaf buds fatten, it feels as though life is bursting out around us. It is. As the sky brightens and birds begin to cry out in defence of their territory and call out for a mate, it feels as though life is beginning again. It is.

And if we sense a lifting of our spirits, a rise in our energy, a flutter of excitement and a new start, that's because spring happens inside us too - not only in our steps but in our minds and hearts.

And because spring is so springy, it can feel out of control so we hear the gardener's cry: 'The bulbs are coming up too soon. I never planted those daffodils there and where has the hellebore gone?

We, too, never know when spring is going to surprise us with a sharp little shoot of hope or the germination of a new idea but let's never try to bury them or push them down. Springs don't like being forced into boxes. Instead, like a good gardener, let's give them a bit of space and nourishment and wait and see what grows.

And if we do feel a sudden spring in our step, let's be thankful and walk sprightly and brightly onward.

New life in the garden
Arnie Rainbow

'Would you like to see the garden?' said the estate agent as we stood on the small patio by the front door.

I was stunned. The house was a Victorian, two-up, two-down, end-of-terrace beside the River Dove. Like most of the local houses, it had been built by the owners of the nearby water mill: Quaker brothers who, clearly, had taken good care of their workforce. But it lacked a real garden. I had already resigned myself to making do with a few potted plants as the divorce settlement had left me with only a modest budget. At least it would give me a new start.

The estate agent escorted me across a footbridge spanning the nearby millstream. He turned and pointed to an unkempt tract of land bounded by the water to the left and a steep wooded bank to the right. The nettles were so high that I could not see the main river but I knew it must be at the far end of the wilderness.

'How much of this would be mine?' I enquired nervously.
'Oh, all of it. It used to be three allotments for the mill-workers but it fell out of use and the mill owner sold it off. The locals tell me it hasn't been worked for nigh on twenty years.'
'Clearly!' I thought. 'Nature abhors a vacuum'.

I felt a twinge of panic but my mind was already shifting into problem-solving mode. It was a river valley, a potential frost pocket. Nettles meant fertile soil; brambles and butterbur would need at least two applications of *Round Up*. It was already spring so I needed to crack on or miss a whole growing season.
Then I noticed an area sheeted over with black polythene,

presumably to stop weed growth. 'There's my starting point,' I thought.

The owners were anxious to sell. I was keen to buy so, two months before completion, I pulled back that black polythene so a friend could rotavate the lifeless, compacted soil. By the time I moved in, I was close to cutting my first cabbage.

For the first few months, I made early starts on my new plot. I saw my first kingfisher, flashing along the millstream, and watched a mother moorhen raising her clutch of chicks, like little balls of black fluff with red beaks. But where were the robins and blackbirds that had always been my gardening companions, snatching up worms and other tasty morsels to feed their little ones? My new garden had trees and undergrowth aplenty for nesting and roosting but, sadly, the soil was devoid of worms and other life. Years of suffocation had taken its toll.

A few years of TLC made all the difference, however, bringing back the worms and, with them, the robins and blackbirds. Now, after a rain shower, they provide a heavenly chorus, sometimes so raucous that I have to switch off my hearing aids so that I can hear myself think!

'Man hurts, nature heals,' goes the old saying. Every time I visit my garden, I marvel that, like my soil, I have been given new life - more than I ever expected - in my 'little Eden'.

Beautiful moment
Mary Martin

Spring is approaching,
bringing steadfast hope, good cheer
and a chance for change.

Entwined branches are swinging
in time to the warm breeze
as gentle buds appear.

Daffodils sway gracefully, beautifully,
some already opened
like a duck's wide beak.

Birds eagerly sing praises,
tweeting songs of unity,
pleasurable music to our ears.

Crunch of acorns beneath our feet.
distinctive smell of being outdoors
adds spring to our steps.

God's magnificent creation,
absolutely remarkable,
pure delight,

if we only take a moment
to be still
and admire the beauty.

New life after death
Margaret Stevens

We are just emerging from the death, decay and darkness of winter which many find hard. We are relieved when we see signs of new life: daffodils, blossom and green buds bursting forth.

What other examples are there? The caterpillar enters the darkness of the cocoon and its body is completely broken down before it is re-formed and emerges as a beautiful butterfly.

And then there are seeds. Seeds have to fall into the ground and be buried. As long as seeds remain in the packet, nothing will happen. But, if they are buried, they will come to life, shooting up, growing and maturing, perhaps producing beautiful flowers and fruits. Each seed will produce not just one flower or fruit, but a rich harvest.

In these examples, there are glimpses and signs, amidst the dying, of the new life to come. Next year's buds can be seen even *before* the old leaves fall off the trees in autumn; the markings on the cocoon *already* show the shape of the butterfly's wings and body; the root shoot is hidden in the seed. Next time you eat peanuts, first break one in half and look for the perfect, tiny shoot waiting to grow.

This is God's pattern but there is a condition: the letting go of the old. There is a death to be gone through first. As Jesus explained, *'Anyone who tries to hold onto his life will lose it; but anyone who lets go will save it.'* Life springs up and grows where the bearers of life don't clutch it to themselves. It is a process of abandonment, losing control, perhaps losing your way, falling or letting go in the darkness.

It's not a process which God inflicts on his creation while he stands back and watches. It is a process which God himself, in Jesus, has gone through, experienced and transformed. It is, however, a painful process. Jesus let go of life. And for three days, death had power over even God.

Unless you fall and die..... let go and lose......

..... you will not live, or be transformed

Our hope of new life after death springs not just from nature. Jesus's death was *not* the end of the story. Spring comes after winter; the seed buried in the ground sends up a new shoot; the butterfly emerges from the cocoon - and Easter follows Good Friday. God's power is greater than death and raised Jesus from the tomb. Any death is the gateway to new life.

I tell you the truth, unless a grain of wheat falls to the ground
and dies, it remains only a single seed.
But if it dies, it produces many seeds...
(John 12:23-25)

Spring in lockdown
Sharon Fishwick

A warm sun shining
Flowers dancing in the wind
Birds welcome the dawn

Nature takes advantage
No humans to compete with
A spring in lockdown

Cars and flights grounded
Ozone holes repair, birds sing,
Nature thrives again.

Liminal space
Nicola Wong

On the edge of burnout or in liminal space?
Betwixt and between, still in the old and waiting for the new.
Joining the dance of creation as
it weaves new threads into a tapestry of life.
The inner state of perceiving, we enter a new way of living.
In transition.

Blessed and graced but not always known or felt.
Not certain, we are challenged out of our old ways
into a new dawn, a new day.
We are vulnerable, empty and receptive,
waiting to be filled with water and turned into new wine
fit for the great banquet, the wedding feast.

Bubbling like a spring in dry ground
to run over and join the river and the ocean with all life.
Sparkling diamonds, glinting from the noonday sun.
Effervescent, effortless, flying free,
the eagle takes to flight and swoops,
then rises again on thermals.

> Wake up, O sleeper and rise from the dead.
> Let us all arise, O Christ of the mysteries.
> Burn away the old, the dross.
> Let us learn afresh from old ways for a new beginning.
>
> The winter is passed, the spring is here.
> Come to me my bride. I AM your lover.
> I come to bless and minister LIFE.
> Live it with me that we may redeem together. Amen

'Silent Spring'?
Arnie Rainbow

'Dad, your birds ain't half noisy!'

I was planting potatoes when my younger son, John, called me on my mobile phone. My plot is beside the River Dove, with lots of undergrowth: a wild-life paradise. An overnight shower had lifted the blackbirds and thrushes into tuneful ecstasy, ably supported by robins, wrens, willow warblers and some 'little brown jobs' (I'm no ornithologist). They were all busy courting and nesting, full of the joys of spring, so much so that I had removed my hearing aids so I could hear myself think!

At such times I am reminded of the best-selling book, *Silent Spring* (1962) by Rachel Carson, a pioneering, environmental text that 'changed the world' by exposing the sinister, cumulative effects of the insecticide DDT (since banned) on wild-life, including the birds and bees! She was my first eco-hero, long before David Attenborough challenged us to think more deeply about our impact on planet Earth, notably on its climate, its forests and its seas. I regard both authors as latter day prophets, issuing wake-up calls, challenging national leaders and corporation tycoons for the greater good.

Until the affluent half of the world embraces a level of responsibility, justice and sharing, implicit in the words of Jesus

Christ: *'Love your neighbour as yourself'* (Luke 10:27), we will do little more than scratch the surface of these problems – especially while some national leaders live in a state of selfish denial.

We read in Genesis that God was pleased with the world He had created. He also made mankind responsible for its welfare. That doesn't mean we shouldn't progress – far from it - but 'progress' is not the same as ruthless exploitation and over-consumption. As Jesus said, *'For what shall it profit a man, if he shall gain the whole world, but lose his soul?'* (Mark 8:36)

Turning back to my garden though, I have to say that spring would be lost without bird song.

New life
Rachel Kenning

It begins as a race, contestants swimming to their destination
but only one will win the prize and be involved in the creation
of new life as they blindly swim through a dark canal.

A sudden momentary explosion of colours at the fusion,
when two become one. A tiny solitary cell, fertilised,
picked up by a hovering tube, drawn into billowing folds,

bubbles and wriggles to divide and become two,
then split again and multiply. The body, just a tail and head
with folds that meet and fuse to form the neural tube,

grows within the sanctuary of the mother's womb,
her constant bounding pulse making it a noisy home.
Placenta surging, murmuring, primitive reflexes responding

until finally the miracle of birth occurs. The baby emerges
from a contracting dark tunnel, dependent and vulnerable.
The life line is cut, the baby is alone.

What a shock! - exploding light and smells and taste,
cacophony of sounds, skin to skin contact.
In response the baby cries, receives life-giving milk.

The race for life has ended, a journey has begun
from darkness into light and warmth, new creation nurtured,
a blossoming of love held in God's hands.

Spring flowers
by April McIntyre

Pushing through cold earth,
gentle snowdrops defiantly
proclaim the spring.

Daffodils laugh
at ever-changing skies of grey,
choosing life.

Deep-scented bluebells,
sheltering in silent retreat,
breathe life's mystery.

Purple waves engulf
rockeries' dying remnants
as life moves on.

Softly-shaded blossom,
branches etching bright blue skies,
heaven-scented.

Osteospermum
opens contemplative petals,
worshipping the sun.

Irresistible spring progress
urges us to put our trust
in resurrection.

It's springtime!
Raymond Lunt

The daffodils trumpet the announcement. Bird song fills the fresh morning air. Blossom colours the tree-lined avenues. The sun seems warmer now as the days have lengthened and, yes, the weeds have awakened, too. It's springtime! A time for new life is here.

When I lived in Cheshire, there was a place always worthy of a visit in the spring. It had been nicknamed 'Daffodil Dell': a stretch of woodland which, in winter months, was dull, dark, boggy and lifeless. But when springtime came, it was transformed into a vast carpet of yellow beneath the freshly budding boughs.

Passiontide and Easter take us through the contrasts of the darkness of betrayal, suffering and sacrifice to the bursting forth of glorious resurrection life. A springtime in the heart becomes possible and new faith and new life can be awakened.

One place where that encounter may be found is in the reading of the gospels in the Bible. They tell the story of the Jesus of history but, through them, God's Spirit can make possible an encounter with the Christ of faith.

During a visit to the Holy Land, we walked the Via Dolorosa, the way of the cross but then, on the Sunday morning, we worshipped at the Garden Tomb. There, amidst the beauty of the garden, close to an ancient tomb hewn out in the rock, we stood to sing:

> *Thine be the glory, risen conquering Son;*
> *Endless is the victory, Thou o'er death hast won.*

It wasn't Easter at the time but, actually, because Christ is risen, every Sunday is Easter Sunday.

This Easter faith in the risen Christ gives birth to new life, inspiring new attitudes towards each other, and new hope, peace and love in the world – another springtime!

A kind of awakening
Eirene Palmer

I like to think of spring as a kind of awakening. I'm not much of a gardener myself but even I can see little buds beginning to protrude from branches and crocuses poking their heads above the ground and saying 'hello' to the world. It's as if God turns on some celestial switch which alerts nature to the fact that winter, with its dark nights and cold days, is behind us and we can look forward to warmth and sunshine.

Faith can be a bit like that. I grew up in a Christian household but can't honestly say that I felt much of a relationship with the Creator of the Universe, or God, or Jesus or whatever name you use, until I was about twelve. I was in my local parish church choir, singing, in true Anglican tradition, the Te Deum, the Jubilate, Venite, Benedicite, Magnificat and Nunc Dimittis, week after week. The words became as familiar to me as my school timetable and my teachers' names. They settled themselves comfortably into my psyche.

Then, imperceptibly, unbidden, the words began to come alive for me and dance. The name of Jesus sent a small thrill down my spine. I couldn't talk about this. The ladies of the choir certainly would have been slightly alarmed at any such revelations and the vicar was a remote figure who I'd never seen in anything but a black wool suit and a white dog collar so big it looked like a dinner plate encircling his neck. Anyway, he might wonder where I had been with God all this time and I couldn't admit that I'd never really struck up much of a conversation.

Yet, like a gardener in the springtime, I nurtured this little shoot of connection and kept watch over it through years and years of its flowering. Sometimes the weather was really rough and it would retreat for a while, to keep itself safe from being battered by storms. Other times, it would flourish and raise its head high and bask in the glorious light. But it grew steadily and constantly, reaching for the sun.

Faith can be like that. It doesn't have to be a revelation of a single moment in time. If the seed is planted, then just trust that it will grow. God, the gentle and wise gardener, will do the rest.

Spring in my steps
Mary Mills

My dog has bad legs and cannot walk fast, or far, so an ambling sniff around my small but lovely South Derbyshire village takes about an hour. This gives me plenty of time for reflection and, one sunny April day in 2020, during the Coronavirus pandemic, it hit me forcibly how blessed I was to live in such a beautiful place that I had under-appreciated! Enhanced by trees in blossom, the heavy scent of hawthorn flowers and new life springing up all around made me appreciate my surroundings much more. One positive benefit of daily walks during Lockdown!

On this particular day, Psalm 23 seemed to come alive, right where I lived.

I am surrounded by green pastures, many with grazing sheep. At the end of the lane is a beautiful horseshoe bend of the River Trent. Water birds abounded – swans, ducks, herons, Canada geese - and once I spotted a kingfisher!

As I stood and gazed, the words of an old hymn I love sprang to mind:

> *When peace like a river attendeth my way,*
> *When sorrows like sea billows roll.*
> *Whatever my lot, Thou hast taught me to say*
> *'It is well, it is well with my soul!'*

During the Coronavirus pandemic, we were all 'walking through the valley of the shadow of death' yet I did not 'fear evil'. I knew, without a shadow of a doubt, that my Good

Shepherd was with me, guarding, guiding all the way. A feast of beauty was provided, even in the presence of the COVID-19 enemy, and a sense of the peace that 'passes understanding'. I knew that, whether I be taken Home to heaven or spared, I would 'dwell in the house of the Lord, **forever,**'

What an amazing truth for every believer!

My soul was restored! It felt good to be alive on such a sunny Spring day and I thanked God for his unfailing love, care and provision for my body, mind and soul.

Surely goodness and mercy **will** follow me all the days of my life.

Thank you, Lord (and thank you, King David) for sharing these 'Good Shepherd timeless insights' – as true today as they were when you composed them thousands of years ago!

Hallelujah! Amen!

Camping in spring
Rachel Kenning

4.30 am. I am woken by a cuckoo.

I've not heard a cuckoo since we were here two years ago and I feel a tingle of excitement down my spine. As the dawn chorus gradually reaches a crescendo, as a cockerel calls across the valley and sheep and lambs bleat in the meadow, I am filled with happiness to be here. Spring has arrived.

Our camp site is set in woodland on the site of an old prisoner of war camp. As I leave the tent, I look up at a circle of blue sky surrounded by the delicate leaves of the silver birches. Below grows a carpet of bluebells. On the edge of the site, rhododendrons are about to bloom. We think there may be mistletoe growing on some of the trees. Catkins dangle from others. It won't be long before the garlic flowers appear and we can breathe in their strong aroma.

Later, we walk through archways of may, avenues of hedgerows bedecked with blossom, verges of lacy cow parsley, the bluebells and dandelions all vying for attention. We pass sheep and lambs grazing in the nearby churchyard and stop at a bridge to look at ducks in the water before going down the track to a park. In the distance, the grass looks completely white and we soon discover that it is covered with daisies.

Canadian geese, with their babies, and swans are nibbling the grass. Beyond the grassland is a lake on which more swans and geese glide. We hear the call of a buzzard and look up to see it circling above us until it is chased away by a crow. We return along a lane where a red-edged triangle warns of the presence of toads.

As night falls, I hear the eerie sound of an owl hooting, followed by the reply from its mate. I snuggle down in my sleeping bag, eagerly awaiting the call of the cuckoo again, filled with warmth and joy at our closeness to creation.

Silver Mount in spring
Sharon Fishwick

An emerging calf glides into rough heather
her first breath of air gasped eagerly,
eyes open, searching to find a warm nipple
full of nourishing milk to warm her belly.

A morning haze spreads over
the rugged white granite tops.
'Welcome, little one, to God's
special world, just for you.'

She slips on wet ground, stands quickly.
but there are no predators now.
Humans and dogs stay at home.
Our lands are safe to roam.

The herd gathers, ready to move on.
Calves ready to run alongside their mothers.
Brae berries, lichen and rich milk,
plentiful food to explore and grow.

Summer

Childhood summers
Rachel Kenning

When I taught childcare courses, I always asked the students what their favourite childhood memories were. The reply was almost always imaginative outdoor play.

Most of my friends and I were children during the 1960's when we had freedom to play in the fields and go for walks on dry and sunny summer days. My happiest memories of summer were those unsupervised hours spent amongst cows and wild flowers, damming the stream near our house, paddling in 'deep' water and catching fish. I also camped in the garden, before joining the Girl Guides and camping for real. I played in our sandpit or swung on a swing under the shade of an apple tree. Dappled shadows; smells of summer flowers; the sweet breath of newborn calves; sounds of a babbling brook and bird song – these are so evocative of my childhood summers.

Of course, most children enjoy summer but it's amazing to see how many of those with special needs become different, much happier, children when outdoors. This has led to a surge in outdoor learning for all children, regardless of the season.

I believe the happiness people derive from being outdoors is due to a spiritual connection between us and the earth. Here, we can be free to express ourselves more fully, and learn so much through observing changes in nature and seasons, in touch with our Creator.

If we have children with us, we are able to learn even more by seeing things from their height and perspective.

The light mornings and evenings and the warmer, sunnier days of summer seem to make us more carefree and relaxed, allowing us to re-charge our immune systems in readiness for the winter. For many, the Covid-19 lockdowns of 2020/21 have ensured a slowing down to appreciate these God-given things.

Looking forward to Summer 2020
Amanda Cartwright

When a breath-borne virus made looking forward to summer a distant memory, I breathed a sigh of resignation and put away my rail card, National Trust card and passport. These 'keys' unlock so much longed-for summer promise before the world turns again to its task of dying down and settling into darkness.

Those plasticised pieces of paper and card are the keys which unlock longed for promises: lunch with brother and sister; afternoon tea with friends; beer and quizzes with grown up children; cool wine at hot pavement cafes and seaside ice cream. How can these keys fail so completely? Defeated by a breath-borne virus, I breathed an exasperated sigh and stoically pretended that Zoom meetings are as good as the yearned for hugs and shared sand under our feet.

Looking away from these paper keys to freedom, I saw, instead, paper rainbows shining from locked windows and doors. With a start and a sharp indrawn breath, I remembered an older promise: a colourful arc set in the sky as a sign that life will continue, that as long as the earth lasts, seedtime and harvest, cold and heat, summer and winter, day and night, shall not cease. That ancient promise that *there will always be another summer.*

Breathing slowly, I remembered that God-given breath which unlocks the universe and brings us to life: the breath which was before any virus existed and will be long after this cruel sharing has ceased.

Before and after Covid-19, before and after summer happiness and disappointment, in every breath we take, GOD IS.

Time
Sharon Fishwick

Time to do the things
you never had time for.
Time to talk to neighbours
you never had time to talk to.
Time to discover technology
to watch the Sunday morning service.

Time to listen to the birdsong
and watch butterflies searching for nectar.
Time to watch the flowers bloom
and enjoy their delicate shades of colour.
Time to tidy and trim the borders,
Plant the veg and cut the grass, again!

Time to cook a meal with fresh food
and make bread with fresh yeast.
Time for the barbeque
you meant to have last summer.
Time to enjoy the taste of wine
in the company of loved ones.

Time to say thank you Lord,
for every day you breathe easily.
Time to sit and quietly contemplate
a new beginning, unfolding around us.
Time to rediscover your priorities
and who you really are.

Summertime
Arnie Rainbow

'Summertime and the livin' is easy'.

Well, maybe, according to the song, from the musical *Porgy and Bess*, but not in my garden! Spuds need to be earthed-up; seeds need to be sown and all manner of vegetable plants, from courgette to kale, need to be planted and protected from voracious wood pigeons and pesky caterpillars. But it's a delightful, earthy busyness that gets me engaged with 'nature' - not just growing fruit and veg, much as I love that. It's also about listening to the birds, watching the butterflies and bees, enjoying the wild flowers (some would call them 'weeds'!) and drinking in the enveloping greenness which, at this time of year, is quite intoxicating.

It reminds me of a question asked by my son when he was just a toddler: 'Why are plants green?' What a good question! Although I had been a botany student, I had to look it up to answer him.

Chlorophyll, the green stuff in plants, captures light to drive growth. Now, sunlight comprises many colours, as we see in a rainbow, but plants mainly absorb red light and reflect green light. That's why plants *look* green. Plants use light energy to make sugars using carbon dioxide (the 'greenhouse gas' we hear so much about) and water, releasing oxygen as a waste product. So, apart from making food for animals and people to eat, the process also improves air quality. Indeed, without green plants we would soon die.

Now, if you think that such a doubly beneficial 'green process' is a happy coincidence, did you know that living with green plants, even pot plants in the home or work-place, also makes us feel better: calmer, less stressed, more relaxed? This is not an old wives tale but is based on solid research. Further research has shown that 'difficult' children are better-behaved and happier after playing in green places, especially amongst trees. After all, what child doesn't enjoy climbing trees and building dens!

More coincidence? I'd call it amazing, intelligent, miraculous design! And it's one of the miracles that pulled this rusty, botany student out of apathetic disbelief and into faith: faith in a creative, caring God.

Oh, one final thought. If plants used the *whole* of the sunlight spectrum, they would look black, not green. Now, there's a thought to reflect on in the summer sunshine!

Open garden Sunday
Raymond Lunt

It's 'Open Garden Sunday'
at Milkington-on-Sea,
the visitors are viewing
before the strawberry tea.
Charities will benefit
from gifts and entry fees;
it's a seasonal opportunity,
a moment to be seized.

There are water garden features,
shrubs, rockeries and pots,
roses, phlox and pink carnations,
fruits, salads and shallots.
There are gnomes with little barrows
and coloured pebble ways
around the lawns and borders
with colours all ablaze.

Parasols on patios
and chairs upon the lawns,
as tea and scones and butter
are served 'til dusk from dawn.
Then as the evening sun sets
and the visitors depart,
the Open Garden gates are closed
until another season starts.

Each garden tells a story
as nature gets to work
upon the gardener's design
and loving handiwork.

It is a precious partnership,
the human and divine,
from the paradise of Eden
until the end of time.

Summer's evening at Carsington
Rachel Kenning

Sun sparkles on distant water as we walk
past hedgerows on verges of clover,
see egg-and-bacon splashes of bright yellow,
ox eye daisies growing tall.
Approaching our destination, stone sentinels,
bright in the evening sun,
rise upon the hill. We hear
the sound of halyards tinkling against the masts
and wavelets gently lapping the shore,
disappearing in the wind,
while gulls wheel and screech,
swallows dip and dive,
geese congregate round people throwing bread.
Huddling, we watch
with wind-tousled hair, distant rain falling.
Then an arc of colours appears,
reminding us of God's promise that
our beautiful earth will never again be destroyed,
whatever floods and troubles
come our way.

Summer haiku

A flotilla
of Canada geese
glide down stream

Mary Mills

Butterflies dancing
bees chasing golden nectar
warming in the sun

Sharon Fishwick

Holidaying ducks
leisurely check out
local amenities

April McIntyre

In meadows greet the summer
Clare Merry

Summer is there for those who go out to greet it.
It passes by the darkened rooms, blinds shut tight and screens aglow.

The warmth of Sun is sweet upon the skin after days of rain and dull humidity.

The bright smiles of passers-by on country lanes are brighter now – against the backcloth of faceless fear that stalks the towns.

Skylarks sing sweeter now that human melodies have stopped and people forgotten the notes they once knew.

Why is the sky still so blue?
Do the heavens not know what has come to pass on earth?
Not know? Not care?

Maybe they say there's hope: a place not corrupted, not destroyed – a little bit beyond our grasp. A place we cannot lay our hands on to change its colour with our mood.

Little birds tweet hope in trees standing amidst rippling meadows of purple grasses. Butterflies with eyes painted upon their wings flit from flower to flower among the meadow hay.

There are the ears which do not hear and eyes which do not see. They never look up from lurid flashing screens. Twitter kills the soul of those who cannot face the peace of silence.

The silence of the meadow is, in fact, full of sound.
Stop! Take stock of the humming, buzzing, tweeting, chirping: humble, happy sounds of creatures content just to be.

Just to be the way that God intended.
Not asking why? Or who? Or how long?

What matters to me now, is now.

The warmth on my back, the blue sky overhead, the song in my ears, the different shades of colour before my eyes and just to be – a spring in my step as I walk through sunny fields.

True life does not hide in the darkness, but celebrates the day. Life is here – oh, two mating insects have landed on the very page I am writing.

Ode to the summer, sunny warmth, the birds and butterflies, and happy things. Don't let the summer pass you by. Hope is here all around us – for those who greet the summer.

Crimson sunrise
Mary Martin

Crimson sunrise,
fresh summer breeze,
strolling free.
Makes us thankful.

Sunflowers waving
beauty greetings,
blooming for all.
Makes us happy.

In the lake,
ducklings dancing
in harmony.
Makes us grateful.

Creation adorning
the greatness of God,
spectacular grace.
Makes us wonder.

Love unchanging,
unconditional,
holding us always.
Forever.

Water of life
Arnie Rainbow

Have you ever wondered why so many of us buy bottled water? Taste, maybe? Convenience? Probably. The fact that it often costs more, pint-for-pint, than milk doesn't seem to occur to us. In fact, the UK is one of the few countries in Europe to enjoy a water supply that is drinkable straight from the tap. Maybe it was the increase in foreign holidays, where bottled water is the norm, or maybe those little green bottles were just too seductive but, nowadays, if I ask a waiter for a glass of *tap* water, I often get a rather odd look.

In the UK it's easy to take water for granted until we have a summer drought, complete with hose-pipe ban. It makes me wonder at folk in third world countries, who often have to walk miles to obtain water - and often dirty water at that. In some parts of the world, such journeys are getting longer and longer as climate change has disrupted normal patterns of rainfall, causing wells and water holes to dry up.

In Jesus' time it was normal for a community to share a well and it must have been an important place for women to pass the time of day and exchange village gossip. The sight of a woman coming to a well in the afternoon heat, however, would have really got tongues wagging, especially when she was a multiple divorcee. Talking to a man, a stranger and a Jew, would have made it so much worse: 'Has she no shame?'

The Samaritan woman must have been stunned when Jesus approached her. In such a situation a man was usually up to no good but Jesus seemed unlike other men. For one thing, amazingly, He knew all about her and her past life. But He didn't talk down to her as most men would. He showed her compassion and He offered her *living water*, a source of eternal life with which she would never thirst for real love or forgiveness ever again (see John 4: 1-26).

In our world today, where so many are thirsting for justice and hope, this is a truly attractive prospect.

Too hot to move
by April McIntyre

Too hot to move as sunshine blazes,
from a picture-postcard sky;
too hot to mow the too-long lawn,
pull-up invading grasses,
tackle furtive, wilted weeds.
Bees tumble through the lavender and thyme,
forgetting to buzz, their little legs
heavy with plunder, weary of busyness.
A sentinel sparrow chirps staccato updates
as forgotten washing stiffens on the line.
Suddenly, a great tit darts from cover,
steals a seed and is gone.
Hiding beneath a too-big, floppy hat
and glasses, I shrink within
the umbrella's welcome shade,
clutching a long, ice-crammed drink.
Too hot to think, to plan, to scheme;
too hot to do the countless worthy things
massing on my silent laptop;
held in this lemon-scented, summer soup.
Only the daisy flowers of argyranthemum
gaze gladly heavenwards,
swaying, receptive, worshipping,
as the sun blasts down.
But I, too, am grateful
for this chance to sit, without guilt:
content to be in the gentle presence
of my Creator God.
Until the unrelenting sun and shrinking shade
move me, slowly, back in-doors.

Closer to me
Mary Martin

*There are so many exciting things to do in summer
but just being with Jesus is best of all*

Summer's exciting
waking with prayer
bliss to be with Jesus

a fine friend of mine
always on my mind
so special

shouts of praises
warm in his presence
cherished and adored

thrilled to sing aloud
seeking your heart's desire
filled with inner peace

so many things to gain
I can't wait
surprises and greatness

turn Summer to joy
nothing compares with these
vibrant moments

Jesus, closer to me

Last of the summer days
Raymond Lunt

Last of the summer days:
heat haze
hovering over the horizon,
hiding the beyond
and the approach of autumn.

Sunbeams dance on ebbing tide,
gulls glide,
while some wait silently beside
the picnic families
before the autumn term begins.

Holidays of fading dreams,
sun creams,
on bodies tanned and peeling,
end the sleeping days
on borrowed summer beds.

Beach ball games are nearly done:
the fun
almost gone for another year.
So children's shouts of glee
ring out above the sound of sea.

Luggage stands by bedroom doors,
all floors,
collected by the hotel staff
for waiting coaches
and the journey home.

The summer now has almost passed.
The last
hours of pleasure looking at the sea
now over for another season
until a summer dawns next year.

Summer prayer: the gift of silence
Nicola Wong

Let me seek, then, the gift of silence, and poverty, and solitude, where everything I touch is turned into prayer: where the sky is my prayer, the birds are my prayer, the wind in the trees is my prayer, for God is in all. (Thomas Merton)

Gentle summer breeze, gift of God,
blow among the swaying grass.
Cooling my skin, it brushes on,
lifting butterflies as they zigzag over erected fences.
Flitting, they dance upon the gardens,
fleetingly resting to drink the nectar of life.
Help me flow in the gentle breeze of your Spirit,
wherever it may take me.
Show us we are all one, for it is one air we breathe;
one body of many parts.

Maybe I will see my *Painted Lady*
on the wing once more,
who flitted far away, for the flower she loves
has grown again and is coming into bud.
May I too, venture where you lead
into pastures new, where you restore my soul.
And we can be together once again,
the lover and beloved.
For your ways are always good
and beneficial to me.

Even when autumn gusts blow away the dross,
may I remember it is good.
Though winter come, may I trust
new life will blossom and spring will return.
Our ongoing cycle of Life.
You Lord hold all things together.
Thank you that you hold us all
in the palm of your hand.
Lead us into new ways,
new paths of grace and simplicity,

I pray.

Farewell to summer
Sharon Fishwick

Dear Summer, you came in late,
allowing Jack Frost extra time
to curl the new green growth
bursting from the germinating seeds.
The pollinated cherry blossom fell softly to the ground,
tiny new buds struggling to gain weight.
But your strong sunshine renewed growth
and mother nature caught up.
A few showers of rain did little to dampen the spirits
and wonderful growth exerted itself, even the weeds
looked beautiful amongst the ripening crops.

The strawberry wine tastes good this evening
and lavender scent still lingers on the evening breeze
as it ripples through cascading golden leaves.
Apples tumble into the long orchard grass,
nourishing food for the insects and birds.

Summer, you're leaving us now
with your positive energy
to help us survive the cold months ahead.
Thank you for visiting.
Looking forward to your return next year.

With love from
Autumn.

Autumn

Extravagance
Martha White

They appear by ones and twos at first. A couple sit by the front door; one is on the breakfast table in the morning. Then there are a handful, strewn among the shoes; half a dozen on the kitchen counter. Soon there is a bowlful on the window sill, a boxful in the garage. I keep finding them falling out of bags or mixed in with the toy cars.

Every autumn, conkers invade our house. These smooth shiny nuts, freshly stomped out of their craggy casings, are impossible not to collect. My sons swoop on the first ones to fall. A few days later, the ground under the tree at the end of our street is covered with split shells and the boys gather them eagerly, heaping them high. Then one looks up at the tree and says, 'Why does it make so *many*, Mum?'

Autumn is a time when we marvel at the extravagance of the natural world. The hedges are covered in berries, the apple trees are covered with fruit – and our lawns are covered with leaves, which we have to rake into rustling heaps. There is just so much of everything. As Christians, we are also reminded to marvel at the extravagance of God. The God we see in the world around us and read about in the Bible is not a stingy God, reluctantly giving blessings to the few who are good enough. This is a God who 'lavished on us' the riches of his grace (Eph.1: 7-8). God sent his Son Jesus not to the holy and religious but to those who thought they could never be loved at all and he told them that God would throw a party to welcome them home.

So next time you pick up a conker, roll it around your hand for a moment. Remember the amazing abundance of nature and the lavish love of a God who is waiting to welcome us home.

Autumn breeze
leaves the colours of the artist's brush
tossed

Haiku by Nicola Wong

Making Chutney
April McIntyre

Only three more days to go – or is it four? I peer into the cupboard to check the date on the jars. Soon it will be time to sample my chutney.

I made it back in August when the fridge was heavy with bulging, dark green produce from the garden. Courgettes don't freeze too well and there's only so much ratatouille you can cope with so I started making chutney: finely chopping courgettes, apricots and apples; onions that made me cry; vinegar for bite; sugar for sweetness, all stirred together in a mighty pan, permeating the house with eye-watering aromas.

Shopping in large supermarkets, with fruit and vegetables imported all year round, we can lose track of the changing seasons so there's something special in growing and using your own produce. And what can be better than cheering up your Christmas pork pie with tasty home-made chutney? As you eat, it brings back memories of days in the garden, wind and sunshine on your face, working hard, sipping an ice-cold drink, tackling the menace of killer slugs.

That taste of summer does us so much good,

psychologically as well as nutritionally. Wouldn't it be good if we could bottle the good times so that when days are grey and wearisome, we could reach for the jar, unscrew the top and savour the sweetness: the exhilaration of being alive; the comfort of being truly loved; the mystery of God's presence with us.

In times past, such blessings were known as consolations - experiences that are life-enriching, heart-warming, uplifting. Today, people of faith may still take time at the end of the day to reflect on what they are most grateful for, seeking to discern where God is moving in it all.

As autumn colours creep over the landscape and crisp winds chase away summer indolence, perhaps we too should squirrel-away a few consolations, storing them in our hearts and minds to sustain us as darker days close in.

Autumn glory
Raymond Lunt

September sun on shimmering seas,
glistening dew on grassy slopes,
golden leaves on chestnut trees,
greet the start of autumn glory.

Rustic orchards, apple red,
cider presses oozing juice,
wheat and barley baked in bread,
breathe the smells of autumn glory.

Seeds sown along a furrowed line,
maturing grain, filled ears of corn,
love sown and nurtured over time,
maturing now in autumn glory.

Golden threads, connecting years
of wedding vows, tried and proved.
Joys and sorrows, hopes and fears,
tell the tales of autumn glory.

September sunsets, golden cords,
reminders of the passing days
where lovely actions, kindly words
keep fresh with hope life's autumn glory.

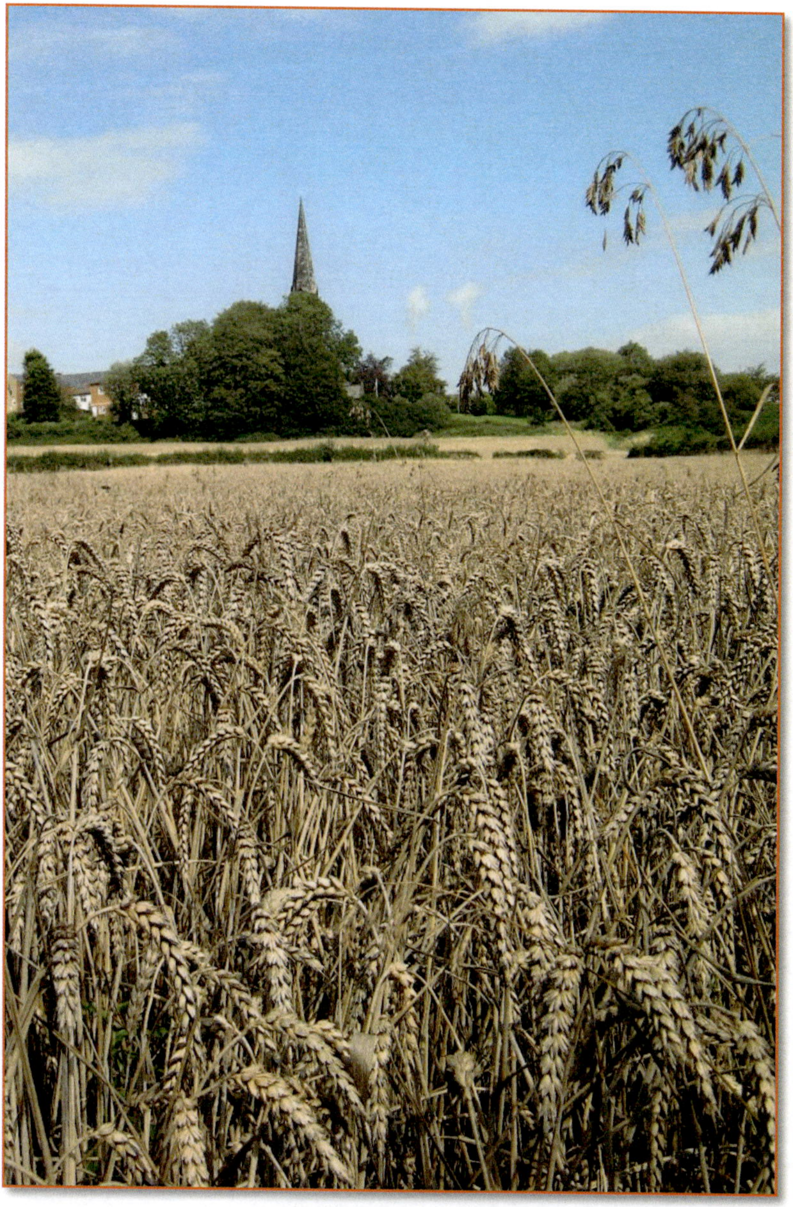

Blessings on the breeze
Rachel Kenning.

A gentle sussuration
of wind in distant trees,
golden rain falling
like blessings on the breeze.
Dew-spangled dawns
of cobwebs spread
transforming hedgerows
to gossamer threads.
Soaring the universe,
the birds of the air
streaking skies with silver,
messengers of prayer.
Berry-dripping branches
stretching up so tall
opening their arms of love
to catch us when we fall.
Time for reflection
beneath autumnal trees,
golden rain falling
like blessings on the breeze.

Geese over the river
Rachel Kenning

Autumn hues tinged the trees. The river shone like copper in the late afternoon sun. Above, some geese flew off but they did not form a perfect 'V' and returned with a great deal of noise, calling to another goose on the water to complete their formation. Despite all their noise, it didn't join them. They didn't know its wings had been clipped and it was unable to fly. So, still imperfect, they travelled in a different direction.

I felt like the goose who was left behind. I knew I was in a rut and felt my wings had been clipped. I also identified with the flock of geese, as if there was something missing. It was time for a change.

My heart's desire was to work with children but instead I was in an easy nine-to-five office job within walking distance of home, happy to plod along in my comfort zone. Then my boss offered me the very appealing opportunity to go on a course which would potentially involve me working in Europe.

I prayed and saw a wooden sign-post surrounded by brambles, symbolizing a cross-roads in my life. One arm pointed to a job working with children in the neighbouring county, the other to Europe. I knew with a sudden clarity that, whichever direction I took, it would be good, leading me to new experiences. I also knew that I had to make the final decision.

For the next few days I felt like the geese, exploring different directions and probably making a great deal of noise when discussing what I should do. Then I followed my heart's desire. I've never looked back wishing I'd taken the other route. I helped to make a difference in many children's lives and met many interesting people.

Autumn may symbolize decay for some but for me it has always meant new beginnings.

Ode to Autumn
Eirene Palmer

'Seasons of mists and mellow fruitfulness' is how John Keats' romantic poem *Ode to Autumn* begins.

I discovered this poem in my teens and loved it – even though it bore little resemblance to 1970's Derby where I was growing up. There weren't many gourds and hazel shells on my council estate and the chief herald of autumn was the beginning of a new school year. I walked the three miles or so to school every day along hard pavements, past rows of houses and corner shops with not a granary or a brook in sight.

But it was still autumn. The trees on my school playing fields shed their leaves as much as any of their country cousins. There was a nip in the air and we were directed to wear our winter uniform of gymslip and woollen V-necked jumper rather than our summer gingham dresses. We had to play hockey instead of tennis - not that that made much difference to me as I was hopeless at both and just ran up and down the side of the pitch or court, trying to look useful.

John Keats had a very different experience of autumn to mine but that is more to do with location than century. Take a hike up into the Derbyshire Dales around September and you will instantly recognise a setting similar to Keats' poem. Both experiences are true but come from entirely different perspectives.

And that set me thinking about how the same thing can look very different, depending on viewpoint. God for instance. For some people, God may come as a Keats' poem, full of imagery and description, romance and beauty, maybe in an instant, a moment of pure experience. For others, God may be hidden, the sense of otherness to be found by walking the backstreets over years and years, recognising, here and there, a sight or sound of something numinous, unexplained. God can be a poem or he can be a lifetime's essay.

It is important to discover your own experience of autumn and not feel pressured into signing up to someone else's. And it's the same with God.

So, let him come to you in your season, in a way that is true – for you. God created us in his image to be truly ourselves.

That's because he loves us so very much.

Conker
Desmond Haigh

Pondering under a Chestnut tree by the church,
like a duckling splashing and exploring,
getting lost in the reeds,
quacking for Mother's guide and comfort,
always there,
when a conker fell down.

Green Velcro flesh cracked open
on stony ground to reddish brown,
with nothing to hold onto or grow
but thoughts of battles gone by
and those to come in conker games
or games of life,
with grazed knuckles and battered hearts.
Raw toxicity of the Chestnut tree
yet extracts healing to inflamed wounds.

I picked up the conker,
bruised by gravity's fall:
a hazelnut in Mother Julian's palm:
God made it; God loves it;
God looks after it.

The church bells rang.
Placing the conker in my pocket,
I floated and waddled into Church.

Downsizing
Ruth Allen

*There is a time for everything,
and a season for every activity under heaven*
Ecclesiastes 3:1

The time has come to downsize our house but where should we start? We've lived here for nearly thirty years and it's a house with lots of storage spaces. Do we have to move? We could put in a stair lift and employ a gardener and a cleaner. There's a local bus stop nearby and shops close at hand. But, no. It's time to go.

Books. I empty a shelf and we decide together, 'Those can go but these we should keep.' Okay. So what's this? Quiz scores inside a *Handbook of Bible Times*. It must have been from a church social group. I remember Claire. She moved away thirty years ago. And Alfred scored highest on the quiz. It makes me smile. We can't have looked at this for thirty years or more. And my teaching books, so brittle and marked with foxing. Time to go.

Clothes. Look at this! I've not been able to get into it for at least seven years. And why have I got ten scarves? Oh, and here's my favourite tee shirt bought on holiday. Why is that still here? And my wedding hat – look how the feathers have disintegrated.

Paperwork. I have kept nearly all my pay slips since I started working. The early ones were actually hand-written! And here are thousands of minutes from various committees, dating back years. Which of these need to be shredded; which need to be passed on? Decisions will have to be made.

The garage. Our car has never even been in it! It's full of things that might come in handy one day. I think we'll need a skip for all this - and help to fill it.

Ecclesiastes 3:6 speaks of *'a time to keep and a time to throw away'*. It's hard to dispose of some things, particularly those which carry sentimental memories; hard to move from the home where our son grew up and so many people have stayed with us. Good days, good memories. But now, as autumn leaves tumble from the trees, swirling and drifting, it seems the right time to let go and 'throw away'. And it's easier than I thought. For God is leading us, through our thoughts and prayers, making even downsizing so much easier.

Weathering the Storm
Arnie Rainbow

Three in the morning. I awoke with a start, trembling, confused. The house was shaking and vibrating. What the hell was happening? Nuclear war? Had some idiot pressed the button? I peeked out through the curtains, half-expecting to see a huge, red glow emanating from London to the south but there was nothing. Thank God!

'Severe gales in East Anglia and South East England are causing widespread damage and disruption to travel,' stated the ever-reliable BBC Radio 4.

It was 16th October 1987. Weather Presenter Michael Fish, he of the natty sports jackets and dashing moustache, who failed to predict this catastrophic storm, has never lived it down. I bet he's been afraid to step into a pub ever since. I was living in Suffolk at the time and know that, at a nearby airfield, the anemometer, which measures wind speed, jammed at 120 miles per hour. I'd say this was not just an autumn gale, Michael, but a hurricane!

A few days later, as I drove by what was left of Rendlesham Forest, I was reminded of my fears about nuclear war. Mile after mile of Corsican Pines were uprooted or snapped in two, an endless landscape of splintered timber and torn foliage. Yet, around the edge, a single line of near-perfect trees stood proud and defiant. But why?

I believe the outermost trees had suffered a life of buffeting so they had grown stronger, with deeper roots and tougher trunks than their over-protected cousins. A counsellor once told me that we grow most during times of pain. Jesus Christ said something similar: *'Blessed are those who mourn for they will be comforted'* (Matt. 5:4).

It took decades to clear the chaos and restore the beauty in Rendlesham Forest but time is a great healer. And with time, even a wounded heart can be healed and strengthened if it is open to love: self-sacrificing, forgiving love.

Pensées
April McIntyre

Growing up in the Potteries, I was used to the smell of turpentine that pervaded our house; used to the sight of a rickety table set out with brushes, colours, palette knife and half-finished ware; familiar with the sight of my mother laboriously painting ceramic jewellery and flower bowls hour after hour, fitting in her job around family life. I remember watching, fascinated, as she painted pansies, delicately shading round the edges of the petals, blending-in the darker blotches, deftly adding the streaks. Perhaps it's why I've always loved pansies.

Cultivated and developed extensively in Victorian times, pansies (from pensées in French) are associated with thoughts and with love. Sown in early autumn, hardy winter varieties will grow and flower as the days shorten, through wind, rain and even snow, splashing their cheer throughout our parks and gardens, faces turned towards the fleeting sun.

What an inspiration! When days are shrouded with autumnal mists and chilly air; when we are wrestling with challenges, uncertain what lies ahead, we can still turn our own faces towards the Son - to the God who loves us, who died for us and who walks with us by his Spirit through summer sunshine and winter storms alike.

And so I remember my mother, in the last years of her life, now painting bookmarks and pebbles to express her faith, turning her gaze towards the God she loved so dearly.

Let us fix our eyes on Jesus ... who for the joy set before him endured the cross. Consider him... (Hebrews 12:2-3)

Changes
Arnie Rainbow

Watching woodland turn to glinting gold, rusty orange and blood red, it struck me how clever Nature is at recycling. As days shorten and frost beckons, valuable nutrients are recovered from the leaves and stored in readiness for the next spring flush of new growth. At the same time, waste products are deposited in the leaves as the trees prepare for winter.

As spent leaves fall to the ground, they feed a vast range of soil life, from fungi to worms which, in turn, provide food for birds and other creatures. The resulting leaf mould enriches the soil and nurtures bluebells, wood anemones and other flowers of the woodland floor. Such is the circle of life – an integral part of Creation, keeping the living world healthy and in balance.

Since the dawn of civilisation, Nature's composting process has been mimicked by mankind, with varying degrees of success. The ancient Chinese were keen recyclers. Centuries of famine made them very frugal and I have them to thank for my own recycling mantra, *'All waste is treasure'* or, as they say in Yorkshire, *'Where there's muck there's brass'*.

For some years, I worked with a variety of composting companies and always wondered at the transformation of garden waste, food scraps and other organic wastes, too unpleasant to detail here, into sweet-smelling, crumbly compost. This compost can inject new life into tired soils and invigorate plant growth and, at the same time, help to protect the planet. This is organic recycling.

A very different form of recycling can be seen in BBC TV's *'Money for Nothing'* programme in which discarded junk, destined for the skip, and worthless, unwanted, items are given a new lease of life, new identity, new value. By contrast, another programme, *'The Repair Shop'*, takes much-loved family treasures and restores and repairs them, taking great care not to change their essential character or purpose. This is 'upcycling'.

Change has always been a vital part of the Christian life. Jesus demanded it, John the Baptist called for it, prophets, like Isaiah, longed for it. Whether we are 'upcycled' or 'recycled', being transformed by God is so fundamental that Christians liken it to being 'born again':

> *'you must be born in a new way before you can see God's kingdom'* (John 3: 3, CEB)
> *'Anyone who belongs to Christ is a new person. The past is forgiven and everything is new'* (2 Corinthians 5: 7 CEB).

I wonder how willing we are to let go and submit to being changed? Something to ponder as the autumn leaves fall and the nights draw in…

As my old RE teacher used to say, 'If you were arrested, charged with being a Christian, and put on trial, would there be enough evidence to convict you?'

Spider!!
Lisa Ollerenshaw

In my kitchen, the other morning, was the largest spider I've ever seen, sitting there on the wall. It was massive: one of those giant garden spiders that can appear when the murky mist droops the autumn leaves as they yellow and fall.

I thought at once of my Dad. Not that he had eight hairy legs but he was always there for me and I could call him anytime for help. He would have moaned a bit, made fun of my wimpiness, then dropped whatever he was doing and come over.

But my Dad is on the other side of the valley of shadow now and I can't reach him (yet).

So, I shakily got out my spider-catcher - a little plastic box on the end of a long stick. The idea is that you put the box over the spider and there's a little trap-door on the base to slide shut.

At this point, my frozen mind finally remembered that I do have a living Father, one that's in me and through me and beside me and with me. So I said a very heartfelt prayer for courage and also prayed that the spider wouldn't run away, which it might well have done when it realized some wobbly muffin was about to put a box over its head. I cautiously advanced.

The God who created the universe, flung stars into space

and has the cares of the world to watch over, obviously heard my prayer and must have sighed, 'Oh, very well then.' I caught my spider without further drama.

This is obviously a very tiny incident in life's rich tapestry but there are times when we all have to face some monster we're really frightened by. I'm talking about proper things such as illness, redundancy or bereavement. Life can be jogging along quite peacefully when suddenly we're standing there, feeling small and vulnerable, with a monster crouched and waiting.

God doesn't make our problems miraculously vanish. No sudden help arrives unexpectedly to take the situation out of our hands. No. The monster (be it illness, job loss or family issues) remains but God stands with us while we face it together. We never have to be alone.

Autumn Prayer
April McIntyre

Seasons changing,
drifting onwards,
letting go of summer with the falling leaves.
We rejoice in each moment of life.

Autumn colours,
splashing God's palette,
radiant inspiration in the burnished sun.
We rejoice in the delight of creativity.

Late harvests,
hedgerow riches,
gathered with wonder and gratitude.
We rejoice in God's goodness and love.

Wild creatures,
active in gardens,
squirreling provisions for harsh, cold days.
We rejoice in our working and our dreams.

Days shorten,
nights draw in,
damp misty mornings, encroaching chill.
We rejoice in the Christ-light, burning within.

Amen.

Remember, remember
Amanda Cartwright

Autumn memories crowd in, bright and clear,
carried on the scent of highly-polished school desks
and crisp new uniforms in September sun,
the oily, greasy, sickly-sweet smell
of a funfair in October's lowering light
and the dank dampness
of bonfire-brightened November darkness.

Surely autumn is the most variegated season,
as colourful as a late and glorious border
and as mixed as the lives it commemorates.

'Remember, remember' is autumn's cry:
remember, remember the flowers of spring and summer
as they now fall to the earth to die and rise again.
Remember, remember history's plots which have moved us on.
Remember, remember the war-ravaged fallen
who died that we might live and think and pray.
Remember, remember, those hallowed ones
who loved us into life,
who we love though they're out of sight
and those nameless saints
who loved the world with Gospel light.

With the dimming of the year,
and the lighting of a candle,
Autumn calls us to remembrance,
when all of our souls are stirred
with the call to new life.

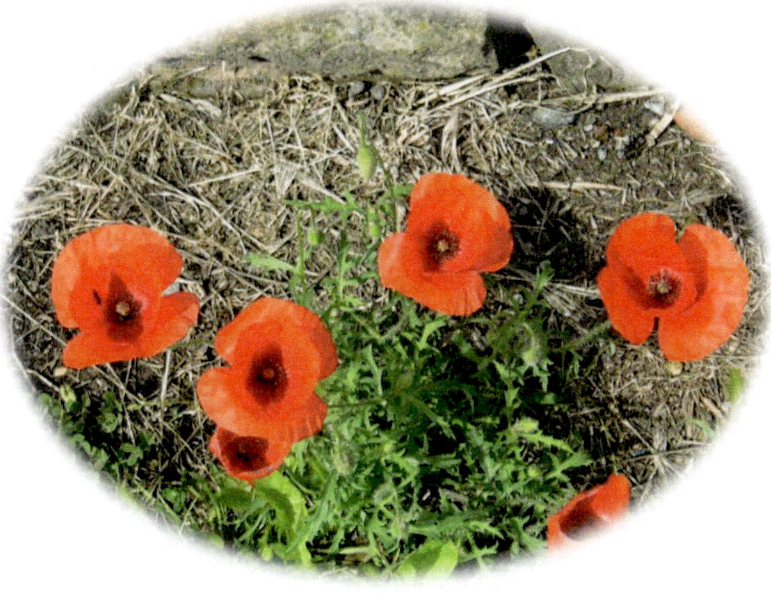

Acknowledgements

Our thanks to all who have contributed to this first collection of work by Café Writers, Derby Cathedral:

Contributors

>Ruth Allen
>
>Maureen Burke
>
>Amanda Cartwright
>
>Sharon Fishwick
>
>Des Haigh
>
>Rachel Kenning
>
>Raymond Lunt
>
>Anna Marley
>
>Mary Martin
>
>April McIntyre
>
>Clare Merry
>
>Mary Mills
>
>Chris Morris
>
>Lisa Ollerenshaw
>
>Eirene Palmer
>
>Richard Palmer
>
>Arnie Rainbow
>
>Christine Statham
>
>Margaret Stevens

Martha White

Nicola Wong

Penny Young

Bible quotations have been taken from The New International Version (NIV) unless stated otherwise

Illustrations contributed by

Sharon Fishwick

April McIntyre

Clare Merry

Richard Palmer

Arnie Rainbow

Christine Statham

Margaret Stevens

Nicola Wong